AF442867

# Are We There Yet? ALL About the Planet Mercury!

## Space for Kids

### Children's Aeronautics & Space Book

BABY PROFESSOR

EDUCATION KIDS

Speedy Publishing LLC

40 E. Main St. #1156

Newark, DE 19711

www.speedypublishing.com

Copyright 2016

All Rights reserved. No part of this book may be reproduced or used in any way or form or by any means whether electronic or mechanical, this means that you cannot record or photocopy any material ideas or tips that are provided in this book

# FACTS ABOUT PLANET MERCURY

Mercury was named
after the Roman
God of Commerce
and TraveL.

Mercury is the
closest planet to
the sun.

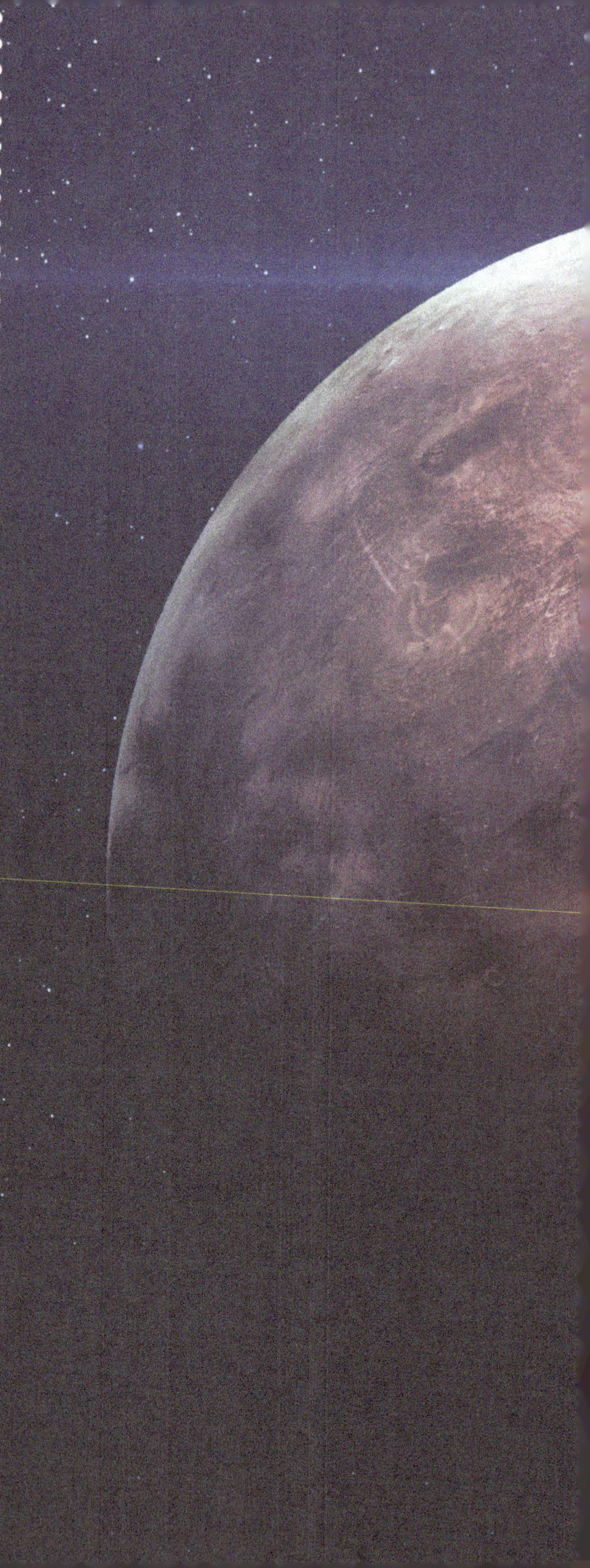

Mercury is the smallest planet in the solar system.

PLanet Earth has
365 days in a year
whiLe mercury only
has 88 days.

UnLike Earth,
Mercury does not
have a moon

UnLike Saturn,
Mercury does not
have rings.

SUN
MERCURY
VENUS
EARTH
MARS
JUPITER
SATURN
URANUS
NEPTUNE

Mercury and our
moon has a similar
surface.

Though Mercury's surface is rough, It stiLL has regions with smooth pLains.

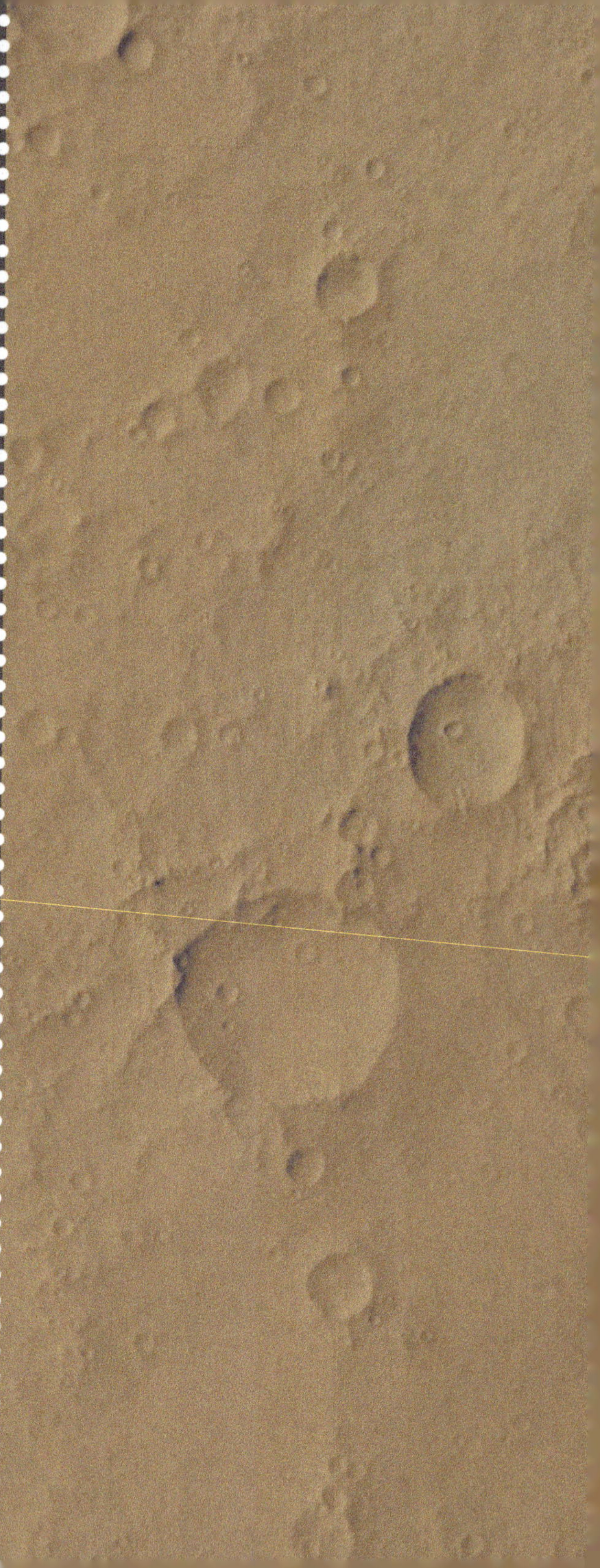

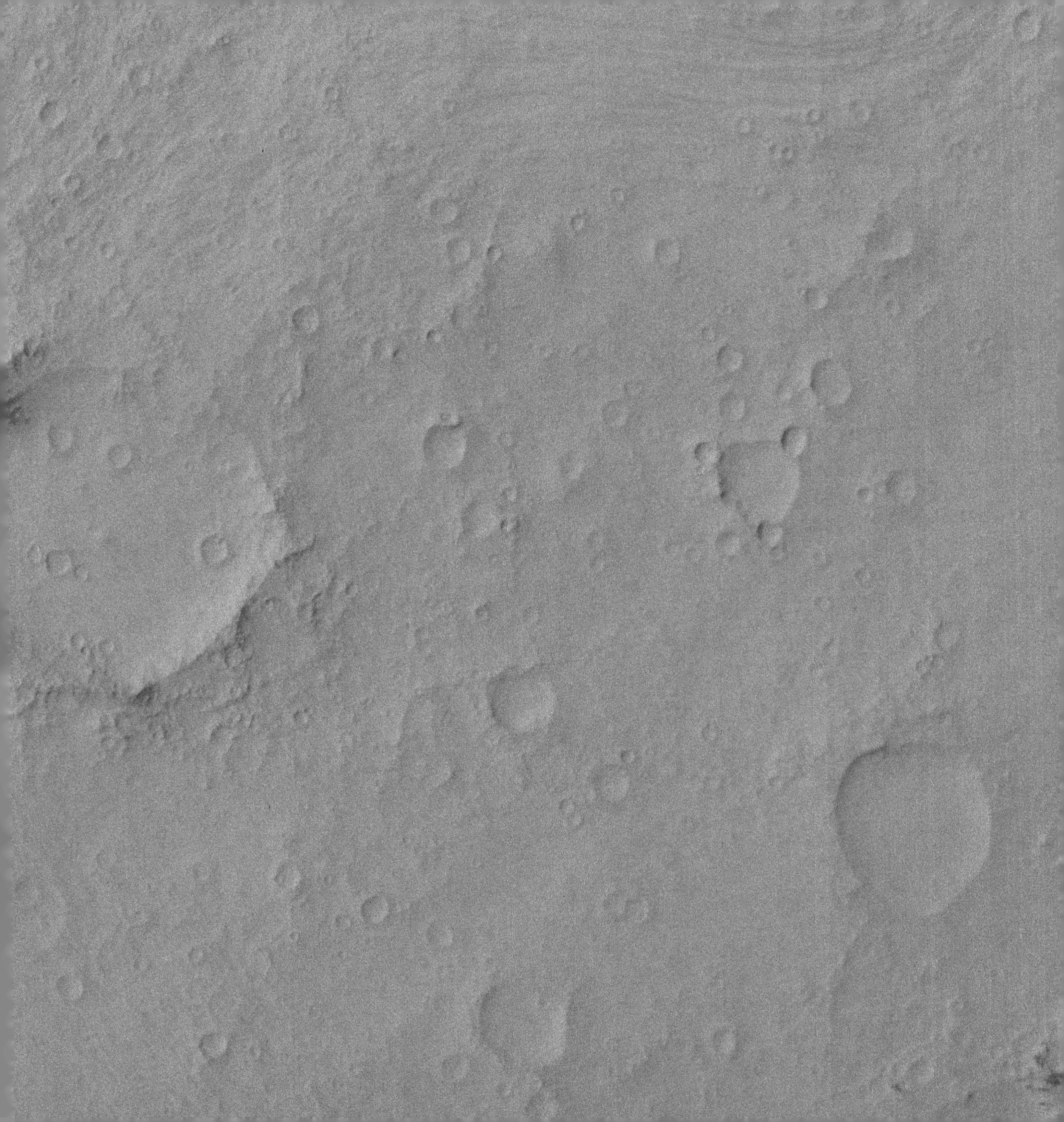

Mercury is the
second densest
planet next to
Earth.

Mercury is the
second hottest
planet next to
Venus.

Mercury does
not have weather
and air because
it does not have
atmosphere.

The surface of
Mercury is full of
wrinkles.

There is no water
in the surface of
Mercury.

Since Mercury
is very near to
the sun, the
temperature is
extremely hot
during daytime.

During night time,
the temperature of
Mercury drops due
to the absence of
an atmosphere.

Just Like Earth,
Mercury has Light
elements Like
sulfur.

Of the 8 planets in
the Solar System,
Mercury has the
most craters.

Mariner 10 is the
first spacecraft to
map Mercury.

Visit
BABY PROFESSOR
EDUCATION KIDS
www.BabyProfessorBooks.com
to download Free Baby Professor eBooks
and view our catalog of new and exciting
Children's Books